D0856002

creatures
of the sea

Killer
Whales

Other titles in the series:

creatures of the sea

Killer Whales

Kris Hirschmann

**KIDHAVEN
PRESS**™

THOMSON

™

GALE

San Diego • Detroit • New York • San Francisco • Cleveland
New Haven, Conn. • Waterville, Maine • London • Munich

For more information, contact
KidHaven Press
27500 Drake Rd.
Farmington Hills, MI 48331-3535
Or you can visit our Internet site at http://www.gale.com

LIBRARY OF CONGRESS CATALOGING-IN-PUBLICATION DATA

Hirschmann, Kris, 1967–
  Killer Whales / by Kris Hirschmann.
    p. cm. — (Creatures of the sea)
Summary: Discusses killer whale anatomy, mating practices, hunting techniques, social structures, and communication.
Includes bibliographical references and index.
  ISBN 0-7377-2058-1
  1. Killer whale—Juvenile literature. [1. Killer whale. 2. Whales.]
  I. Title.
  QL737.C432H586 2004
  599.53'6—dc22

                                                                    2003023205

Printed in the United States

Table of Contents

Name Game

Killer whales have a fierce reputation. This reputation is well deserved. Killer whales are powerful predators that will eat just about anything they can catch, including much larger creatures. Even the mighty blue whale, which may grow to a length of nearly one hundred feet, is not safe from a group of hungry killer whales.

Eighteenth-century whalers saw battles between killer whales and their largest prey. Impressed by the power and ferocity of the killer whale, sailors nicknamed these animals "whale killers." But over time, the nickname got reversed. People started referring to these creatures as "killer whales." The new phrase caught on and soon became the animals' accepted name.

The term *killer whale*, however, is misleading. Although killer whales are related to whales, they are not whales themselves. Instead they are part of the scientific family **Delphinidae**, which includes

Killer whales are powerful predators with a fierce reputation.

dolphins and porpoises. Killer whales are actually the largest members of the dolphin family.

Because *killer whale* is not accurate, many scientists prefer to use the name **orca**. This word is taken from the killer whale's scientific name, *Orcinus orca*. *Orca* comes from a Latin word meaning "the shape of a barrel or cask" and probably refers to the killer whale's body shape. Scientists like this name because it does not have the negative feeling of the word *killer* and it avoids the word *whale* altogether.

In recent years the word *orca* has become more and more common, even in the nonscientific community. But still, the killer whale's original nickname lives on. Perhaps this is because the phrase seems to fit. Killer whales are among the biggest, fiercest, fastest hunters in the ocean.

1

Understanding Orca

Physically speaking, killer whales are impressive animals. Male killer whales, which are called bulls, average 19 to 22 feet from nose to tail and weigh between 8,000 and 12,000 pounds. Females, which are called cows, average 16 to 19 feet in length and 3,000 to 8,000 pounds in weight. The largest male ever recorded was 32 feet long and weighed 22,000 pounds. The largest female was 28 feet long and weighed 16,500 pounds.

No one knows exactly how many of these huge animals roam the world's oceans. Some scientists think there may be several hundred thousand killer whales. Others believe the worldwide killer whale population may be as small as one hundred thousand.

Killer whales live in every ocean of the world, but scientists do not know for sure how many of the animals exist.

Finding Killer Whales

Killer whales live in every ocean in the world. They are most common in cold-water areas, including the Arctic and Antarctic. Large populations live off the chilly coasts of Alaska, Canada, Norway, Iceland, and Argentina. Killer whales can also be seen along the coasts of Great Britain, North Africa, the western United States, and other places where water temperatures stay low year-round.

Although killer whales prefer cold water, they sometimes roam into warmer areas as well. Killer whales have been seen near Hawaii, Australia, the Galápagos Islands, and the Bahamas. They have even been seen in the Mediterranean Sea and the Gulf of Mexico, two very warm bodies of water.

Sometimes killer whales even enter rivers. These animals have been spotted in Oregon's Columbia River, England's Thames River, Germany's Elbe River, and the Netherlands's Rhine River. Scientists think the killer whales probably swam into these rivers to hunt for fish.

Most killer whales do not stay in one area. Instead they constantly travel from place to place. These movements are not migrations, which can be defined as yearly trips from one specific home to another. They are just attempts to find good food sources wherever they may occur. Killer whales that live closest to the earth's poles may also move north or south as the pack ice (a solid frozen covering over the ocean's surface) grows and shrinks with the changing seasons.

Powerful Bodies

Killer whales are built for life on the move. These animals' bodies begin with a tapered snout that cuts easily through the water. From the snout, the body broadens smoothly into a wide head and then a thick, powerful trunk. The trunk tapers again to a slender tail stalk. This sleek shape streamlines the killer whale and helps it to swim easily wherever it goes.

The killer whale's main swimming tool is its powerful tail. The tail ends in two lobes called **flukes,** which are tough, flat pads of boneless tissue. A killer whale uses muscles in its back and tail stalk to wave the flukes up and down in the water. This motion creates a push that shoves the killer

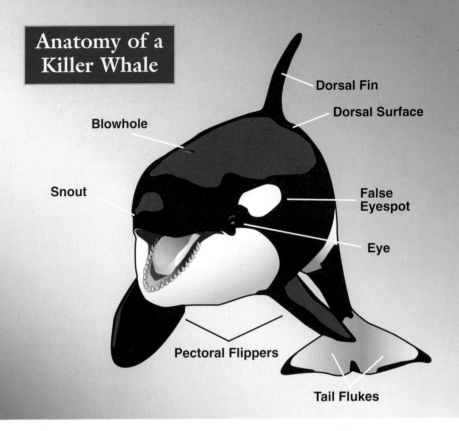

Anatomy of a Killer Whale

Dorsal Fin

Dorsal Surface

Blowhole

Snout

False Eyespot

Eye

Pectoral Flippers

Tail Flukes

whale forward. The push can be very strong. For short distances, a killer whale can swim as fast as thirty miles per hour.

Two **pectoral flippers**, which are found just below and behind the head, also help the killer whale as it swims. The pectoral flippers contain many bones, similar to the bones in a human hand or foot. However, the killer whale cannot move these bones separately. It can only wave each pectoral flipper as one piece. A killer whale uses its pectoral flippers mostly to steer as it glides through the water. It can also twist its flippers to help itself slow down or stop.

The killer whale's final swimming tool is the triangular **dorsal fin** on its back. Like the flukes, the dorsal fin is made of boneless tissue. In males, this fin may be six feet tall—about the height of a human male. This is the tallest dorsal fin of any whale or dolphin species. The mighty fin acts like the keel of a boat to keep the killer whale steady in the water as it swims.

Recognizing Killer Whales

The dorsal fin is not just a swimming aid. It is also one of the killer whale's most recognizable features. Differences in the shape and size of this fin can be used to identify individual killer whales.

The main differences are between male and female killer whales. Males have much taller dorsal fins than females do. (Females' dorsal fins are usually between three and four feet tall.) Males' dorsal fins are also more upright.

The killer whale's most recognizable feature is its dorsal fin.

Dorsal fins of both male and female killer whales may also bear distinct marks. About one-quarter of all killer whales, for example, have bent or curled dorsal fins. Dorsal fins may also be notched or scarred. Scientists can use these markings to help them recognize certain killer whales.

Coloration is another feature that makes killer whales easy to recognize. They are pitch black on their backs, pectoral fins, and upper tails. They have snow-white eye patches and underbellies. They also have a grayish **saddle** located just behind the dorsal fin. The saddle varies in color and shape from one orca to another. Like the shape of the dorsal fin, this feature can be used to identify individuals.

Marine Mammals

Although they spend their entire lives in the water, killer whales are not fish. They are mammals—and like all mammals, they must breathe air to survive. Killer whales breathe through openings called **blowholes** on top of their heads. To get air, a killer whale approaches the surface, breathing out as it goes. It sticks its blowhole out of the water and sucks in a lungful of fresh air. The killer whale then closes its blowhole and arcs smoothly back into the sea.

A killer whale that is swimming near the surface breathes about once every thirty seconds. Orcas can hold their breath longer if they need to dive in search of food. These animals can easily swim underwater for four or five minutes and may even stay

Killer whales frequently swim to the water's surface to breathe.

below for up to fifteen minutes if necessary. However, dives of this length are rare. Killer whales prefer to stay in shallow waters where they can easily get all the air they need, whenever they want it.

Breathing air is not the only feature killer whales share with other mammals. They are also warm-blooded, which means they maintain a constant body temperature between ninety-seven and one hundred degrees Fahrenheit. To keep body heat from escaping into chilly water, killer whales have a three- to four-inch layer of fatty **blubber** just beneath their skin. Blood vessels in the flippers, flukes, and dorsal fin also help to adjust the killer whale's temperature. When the water is cold, these vessels get smaller and prevent warm blood from reaching the skin's surface. This traps heat inside the killer whale's body. When the water is warm, the vessels get larger so blood can flow freely.

Automatic temperature control is just one of many ways the killer whale stays comfortable in its environment. Everything about this animal, in fact, seems to be designed for success in the ocean world. It is no wonder the killer whale rules the seas today, just as it has for millions of years.

chapter 2

Family Matters

Killer whales can have long lives. Although no one is sure exactly how long these animals live, scientists believe females can reach eighty to ninety years of age. Males probably reach just fifty to sixty years. For both males and females, the average life span is usually shorter than this. Most female killer whales live about fifty years, and most males live thirty years or less.

During its lifetime, a killer whale's most important job is creating babies. Mature females usually have one baby every three to five years. Males do their part by mating as often as they can. In this way, adult killer whales make sure that there will always be a new generation of orcas to replace those that die.

Mating Season

Female killer whales are able to mate when they are fifteen to sixteen feet long. They usually reach this length when they are between six and ten years old. Most males reach maturity when they are eighteen to twenty feet long, or between ten and thirteen years old. One sign of male maturity is a growth spurt of the dorsal fin, which does not reach its full height until the orca becomes an adult.

In the mating game, older males have the advantage. Females prefer bigger, stronger males and usually ignore smaller individuals. For this reason, males may not mate for many years after they are physically ready. They must spend some time growing before they are finally able to attract mates.

Breeding season begins when females come into **estrus**. This means they are ready to mate. Females can come into estrus during any season, but summer seems to be the most common time. Males compete to attract the attention of females in estrus by slapping the surface of the water with their flippers and flukes. They may also chase, splash, nudge, and stroke the females. Killer whales have very sensitive skin, and the females seem to enjoy being touched by their male admirers.

After a while, the female chooses a partner. The two animals mate while swimming. When the mating process is over, the female sometimes chooses a new partner and mates again. She may do this several

Killer whales give birth every one to three years.

Male killer whales slap the surface of the water with their flukes to attract females.

times. Mating with many males gives the female more chances to get pregnant.

A Baby Is Born

A pregnant female carries a developing baby inside her body for fifteen to seventeen months. Killer whales usually carry just one baby at a time. Twins have been seen, but they are very rare.

By the time the baby is ready to be born, the mother's underside bulges. The first sign of labor is a small black tail poking out of a slit in the mother's snow-white belly. The mother begins to swim quickly, wriggling and barrel rolling as she goes. These actions help to push the baby, which is called a calf, from the mother's body. Soon the small killer whale bursts into the world amid a cloud of blood.

Right away it swims toward the water's surface to take its first breath of air. The mother helps her calf by nudging it upward with her snout.

Newborn calves are much smaller than their parents. Both males and females are between seven and nine feet long and weigh three to four hundred pounds. Their dorsal fins and flukes are droopy at first, and their light areas are cream colored or pale orange rather than white. A calf's fins and flukes stiffen within a few days. The light areas will take about a year to fade to the brilliant white seen in adults.

A young calf stays near its mother's side. The adult female protects her small baby from sharks or any

After giving birth, mother killer whales nudge their calves to the surface for their first breath of air.

other predators that might attack it. Mother and baby will stay close together until the young killer whale gets big enough and strong enough to look out for itself.

Growing Up

During its first months of life, a killer whale calf survives by drinking milk from its mother's body. The milk comes from nipples that are hidden in slits on the mother's belly. To get milk, a calf presses its tongue against the roof of its mouth to form a tube. The calf then holds its mouth against the mother's body. The mother squirts her milk right down the baby's throat. This process is repeated several times each hour, around the clock.

The female killer whale's milk is very rich. Almost half of the milk content is pure fat. This high-calorie drink helps calves grow quickly. It also helps them build the blubber layer that will keep them warm in their cold ocean home.

When a calf is two or three months old, its upper teeth begin to poke through the gums. Lower teeth erupt about a month later. With its teeth in place, the calf starts to experiment with solid food. Its main food, however, is still its mother's milk. Killer whale calves nurse until they are about one year old. At this time, they are able to eat an adult diet. They are also much larger than they were at birth. By the time a year has passed, most killer

Baby killer whales stay near their mothers until they are big and strong enough to protect themselves.

whale calves have gained about a thousand pounds and have grown several feet in length.

Family Groups

As time goes by, a young killer whale gets better and better at finding its own food. It also gets bigger and stronger, and it does not need its mother's help or protection as it once did. But still, it never leaves its mother's side. A female killer whale, her children (both male and female), and her daughters' children live together throughout their lives in stable families called **maternal groups**. Maternal groups may contain anywhere from three to ten members.

All group members, even the males, help to take care of the youngest killer whales. They train the calves to hunt, communicate, avoid danger, and do

Killer whales live together in maternal groups of three to ten killer whales.

everything else necessary to stay safe in the under-water world. This training gives each calf the best possible chance of surviving to adulthood. But the death rate for killer whale calves is still very high. Between 40 and 50 percent of all orcas die during their first year of life. Of these, many die at birth. Others are killed a little later by predators, diseases, or other causes.

This high death rate is nature's way of making sure only the strongest animals survive. Killer whales that make it through the dangerous first year are tough and healthy. When they reach maturity, they will be able to produce tough, healthy babies of their own. The strongest of these babies will eventually grow up and produce more babies, and the cycle of life will continue.

Top Predators

K iller whales are the ocean's top predators. These powerful hunters are known to eat several hundred different types of animals, including fish, squid, seabirds, sea turtles, seals, sea lions, walruses, otters, penguins, whales, and polar bears. One killer whale was even found with the carcass of a moose in its stomach.

Because killer whales are very active, they need a lot of food. An adult killer whale eats about 3 to 4 percent of its body weight in food each day. A growing calf needs to take in as much as 10 percent of its body weight during each twenty-four-hour period. Finding all this food is no problem for the killer whale, which is one of the world's most skilled predators.

Adult killer whales are the ocean's top predators, and they eat hundreds of different kinds of animals.

Finding Food

Killer whales have many ways to find food. The most important way involves a skill called **echolocation**. Echolocation is the use of sound to "see" distant objects. It is similar to the sonar that is used on ships, but it works much better than the best human systems.

To echolocate, a killer whale uses air sacs in its head to produce a fast series of clicking sounds. It sends these clicks out through its forehead, which contains an oil-filled organ called the **melon**. The killer whale uses muscles to change the shape of the melon. This organ acts as a lens to focus the clicks into a tight beam of sound. The beam shoots out in front of the killer whale. When it hits an object, part of the sound bounces back toward the killer whale as an echo. The killer whale receives this echo with its fat-filled lower jawbone. From there, the echo is sent to the brain, which translates the sound into a picture. If the picture shows a fish, a seal, or another tasty animal, the orca may move in for the kill.

Killer whales also have sharp eyesight. Vision is helpful when a killer whale is traveling through clear, calm water during the daytime. It is also useful when killer whales want to spot seals, penguins, or other animals above the water's surface. To find these animals, killer whales simply poke their massive heads out of the water and look around. This behavior is called **spy hopping**.

When a killer whale finds food, it lets the other members of its group know right away. A killer whale might signal by leaping or splashing. It might also make noises to tell other killer whales that food is nearby.

Killer whales have sharp eyesight and will spy hop out of the water to look for prey.

Hunting Techniques

Killer whales usually chase prey in groups. They change their method depending on the circumstances and the prey. When hunting a school of fish, for example, killer whales sometimes use a technique called carousel feeding. In this technique, a group of killer whales swims beneath and around a school of fish to herd it into a tightly packed ball. The killer whales then take turns swimming through the school, smacking the fish with their powerful tails as they go. An orca leaves dozens of dead and stunned fish in its path. It eats the prey, then returns to its herding duties so another killer whale can go on the attack.

Killer whales also use group hunting techniques to overcome large animals, such as whales. Scientists saw one of these attacks in action off the coast of Mexico. About thirty killer whales surrounded a sixty-foot blue whale. The orcas took turns biting chunks of flesh and blubber from the whale's back and sides. They continued their attack for about five hours. Then they swam away, leaving the severely injured whale to die from its wounds.

Sometimes killer whales work together to tip animals off ice floes. In this hunting method, a killer whale spy hops to spot prey that is resting on floating chunks of ice. Then the killer whale swims beneath the edge of the floe. It pushes the edge upward so seals, penguins, or any other creatures

③ *Killer whales hunt in groups and work together to attack prey.*

on the floe slide off the other side—right into the open mouths of more hungry killer whales.

The most spectacular hunting method of all can be seen along the beaches of Punta Norte, Argentina, and the Crozet Islands in the south Indian Ocean. In these areas, killer whales bodysurf onto rocky beaches to seize careless seals and sea lions. With their prey clamped firmly between their jaws, the killer whales wriggle their huge bodies to work their way back into deeper water.

Eating Prey

Once killer whales have caught their prey, they must eat it. To help in the eating process, killer whales have mouths full of cone-shaped teeth. The teeth are one inch across at their base and taper to a rounded point. Each tooth is about three inches long. The number of teeth varies from orca to orca, but most killer whales have between forty and fifty-six teeth. These teeth interlock like the two halves of a zipper to give the killer whale a tight grip on slippery prey.

Killer whales cannot replace their teeth. They get just one set that must last their entire lives. The killer whale's teeth, however, must chew through bones and other tough materials. As a result, the teeth of older killer whales are often broken or worn down from years of use.

Although a killer whale's pointed teeth do not work well for chewing, they are excellent grabbing and ripping tools. A killer whale can easily tear even the largest prey into bite-sized chunks. Usually this is not necessary. A killer whale's mouth and throat are so big that even a small seal or walrus can be swallowed whole. But when a killer whale goes after really large prey, such as a whale, the ability to tear flesh is essential.

All food, whether large or small, is pushed into the throat by the killer whale's large pink tongue. This flexible organ looks much like a human tongue, but it is hundreds of times bigger.

Killer whales have between forty and fifty-six teeth which they use for gripping and tearing.

Safe in the Sea

Adult killer whales have no natural enemies. These animals are so large and powerful that no other creature in the ocean dares to attack them. Even the biggest, hungriest shark is no match for a full-grown killer whale.

Humans are the only creatures on Earth that consistently attack killer whales. In some cultures, killer whale flesh is eaten as food. In other areas, fishermen kill orcas to keep them from eating the local fish. The fishermen worry that a large killer whale population might gobble down their catch and their profits.

Although some killer whales are killed each year by people, these animals are not major targets. Most killer whales live their entire lives without being bothered by human hunters. As a result, there are plenty of killer whales in the world's oceans.

chapter 21

Killer Whale Society

Killer whales are highly social animals. They form close bonds with other killer whales, and they depend on each other for help and support in every area of their lives. This dependence is an important part of the killer whale's success. By working together, groups of killer whales can accomplish things that a single killer whale could not do.

Social Structure

There are three main levels of killer whale society. The basic level is called a **pod**. A pod includes several related maternal groups, and it usually has between ten and twenty members. Pod members travel, hunt, and play together throughout their lives.

Killer whales are highly social animals, and they form close bonds with each other.

Just above the pod is a level called the **clan**. A clan is a group of related pods living in the same general area. All of the killer whales in these pods are thought to be related to each other.

The top level of killer whale society is called the **community**. A community includes all the clans in a region. Pods from the same community sometimes travel together, forming large groups of one hundred members or even more. Mating probably takes place when these large groups, or superpods, come together.

Every group of killer whales, no matter how large or how small, follows a strict social order.

Old, big females are usually the leaders. They tell other killer whales they are in charge by head butting, biting, and scraping their teeth against the skin. Young killer whales often have scratch marks on their skin. These marks show that an orca has been put in its place by one of the group's dominant females.

Residents and Transients

Killer whales follow two main social styles: **resident** and **transient**. By watching a pod's behavior, scientists can easily tell which style the group is following.

Killer whale behavior indicates which social style the pod is following.

The resident style is more common than the transient style. Resident pods can be large, with as many as fifty members (though usually there are fewer). Pod membership is very stable. New members seldom join the group, except by birth, and current members seldom leave. Resident killer whales also tend to roam the same areas over and over. Their movements usually match the migrations of the prey on which they feed.

Resident killer whales eat mostly fish to survive. When hunting, pod members constantly chatter and send out echolocation calls. If the killer whales spot seals or other potential prey animals, they do not usually attack them. Instead they keep looking for fish, which they seem to prefer above all other meals.

Resident killer whale pods are stable and tend to roam the same areas over and over.

Transient killer whales behave much differently from residents. Their pods are smaller, usually having just a few members. Their society is not as stable as that of resident killer whales. Orcas sometimes switch from one transient pod to another, or even strike out on their own. Transient killer whales also have a much larger range than residents and may turn up just about anywhere the search for food takes them.

Although transient killer whales will eat fish, they seem to prefer larger prey. Transient pods work together to find seals, sea lions, walruses, dolphins, and other warm-blooded meals. But instead of using echolocation, as residents do, transient killer whales search silently so they will not be detected. They do not "talk" until after they have made their kill.

Some scientists believe killer whales have a third social style. Killer whales that follow the third style are known as the **offshore** type. Offshore killer whales stay far from land at all times. They form large groups of up to sixty individuals and probably eat fish. Offshore killer whales are very hard to find and study, so not much is known about these animals.

Communication

Killer whales of all types use sound to communicate. Killer whale noises have been described as squeaks, squeals, creaks, whistles, and groans. To make these

Killer whales use many types of sounds to communicate with each other.

noises, killer whales use the same air sacs in their heads that produce echolocation clicks. But they do not shoot the sounds forward in a beam, as they do when echolocating.

Different killer whale pods have different **dialects**, or ways of "speaking." Resident pods usually have about twenty different calls that they use over and over. Transients have only five or six different calls. All pod members use calls from their specific dialect when they communicate with each other. The calls of nearby pods are similar, but not exactly the same, and the sounds made by distant pods are quite different. Scientists believe that pods with very similar dialects are closely related. Those whose dialects are completely different probably are not related at all.

A killer whale's noises are not a language in the human sense, with certain sounds attached to certain meanings. However, killer whales can communicate many general things through sound. For example, they can tell other killer whales where they are. They can warn pod members of danger or whistle to tell them that food is nearby. They can ask for attention or signal other killer whales to back off. Scientists believe that killer whales can even recognize each other's voices. So when a killer whale makes noise, it is not just communicating mood, location, and other general ideas. It is also telling its pod members who it is.

Display Behavior

Killer whales do not communicate only with sound. They also "talk" through spectacular athletic displays. In one such display, a killer whale leaps high above the water's surface, then lands on its back or side. This behavior is called **breaching**. A breaching killer whale creates a huge splash and a loud noise. By doing this, it shows other killer whales how big and strong it is.

Other killer whale displays include **lobtailing** and **fin slapping**. In lobtailing, a killer whale lifts its flukes out of the water, then smacks them loudly on the ocean surface. In fin slapping, a killer whale slaps either its dorsal fin or pectoral flippers against the surface. These behaviors are not as spectacular as breaching, but they do make noise. Scientists believe

Killer whales communicate with each other through behavior such as breaching.

that lobtailing and fin slapping are other ways of showing dominance. During breeding season, these behaviors may also be used to attract mates.

Sometimes killer whales leap out of the water for no apparent reason. They may also corkscrew their bodies in the water and chase each other. Scientists who have seen killer whales acting this way think there is only one explanation for their behavior. They are sure that the killer whales are playing with each other. Is this a sign of intelligence? No one knows for sure. But killer whales are, after all, dolphins proba bly the smartest creatures on Earth after humans. As members of the dolphin family, killer whales certainly get high marks in the brains category. Intelligence is just one of many features that make killer whales successful in their ocean home.

Glossary

blowhole: A hole on the head through which the killer whale breathes.

blubber: A thick layer of fat that lies just beneath the killer whale's skin.

breaching: Leaping out of the water and making a big splash.

clan: A group of related pods living in the same general area.

community: All the clans that live in a region.

Delphinidae: The scientific family to which killer whales belong.

dialect: The pattern of sounds used by a certain pod.

dorsal fin: A triangular fin on the killer whale's back.

echolocation: The ability to "see" with sound. Sound waves are sent out, and the returning echoes are interpreted.

estrus: Readiness to mate.

fin slapping: Smacking the dorsal fin or pectoral flippers on the water's surface.

flukes: Flattened pads of tough tissue at the end of the killer whale's tail.

lobtailing: Slapping the flukes on the water's surface.

maternal group: A stable family group consisting of a female killer whale, her children, and her daughters' children.

melon: An oil-filled organ in the killer whale's head that directs sound waves.

offshore: A type of killer whale that stays in the open ocean.

orca: Another name for the killer whale.

Orcinus orca: The scientific name given to all killer whales.

pectoral flippers: Two flippers just behind and to the bottom of the killer whale's head.

pod: Several related maternal groups of killer whales.

resident: A killer whale that lives in a stable pod, eats mostly fish, and roams a predictable territory.

saddle: A gray area just behind the killer whale's dorsal fin.

spy hopping: Poking the head out of the water to look around.

transient: A killer whale that changes pods frequently, eats mostly marine mammals, and travels unpredictably.

For Further Exploration

Books

Linda Moore Kurth, *Keiko's Story: A Killer Whale Goes Home*. Brookfield, CT: Twenty-First Century Books, 2000. Describes efforts to return Keiko, orca star of the movie *Free Willy*, to the wild.

James G. Mead, *Whales and Dolphins in Question: The Smithsonian Answer Book*. Washington, DC: Smithsonian Institution Press, 2002. The Smithsonian's National Museum of Natural History receives thousands of questions each year about whales and dolphins. This book asks, then answers, the most common questions.

Jane Resnick, *All About Training Shamu*. Bridgeport, CT: Third Story Books, 1994. Read about the techniques used to train Shamu and other killer whales at Sea World marine parks.

Roland Smith, *Whales, Dolphins, and Porpoises in the Zoo*. Brookfield, CT: Millbrook Press, 1994. This book explains why zoos keep whales, dolphins, and porpoises. It also describes how zoos treat and manage these animals.

Adam Woog, *Killer Whales.* San Diego, CA: Kid-Haven Press, 2001. Take an in-depth look at the hunting habits of killer whales around the world.

Websites

Jean-Michel Cousteau's Ocean Futures Society, (www.oceanfutures.org). This site includes up-to-the-minute reports on Keiko's condition and activities.

Killer Whales (www.abc-kid.com). This site includes page after page of great killer whale photographs.

Index

picture credits

about the author

Kris Hirschmann has written more than ninety books for children. She is the president of The Wordshop, a business that provides a variety of writing and editorial services. She holds a bachelor's degree in psychology from Dartmouth College in Hanover, New Hampshire. Hirschmann lives just outside Orlando, Florida, with her husband, Michael, and her daughter, Nikki.